WAITING FOR GOD

A Play in Two Acts

by Michael Aitkens

SAMUEL FRENCH

samuelfrench.co.uk

ISBN 978-0-573-11635-3

www.samuelfrench.co.uk
www.samuelfrench.com

For Amateur Production Enquiries

United Kingdom and World
excluding North America
plays@samuelfrench.co.uk
020 7255 4302/01

Each title is subject to availability from Samuel French, depending upon country of performance.

MUSIC USE NOTE

USE OF COPYRIGHT MUSIC

IMPORTANT BILLING AND CREDIT REQUIREMENTS

ABOUT THE AUTHOR

Michael has worked all over the world and has had over two hundred scripts produced for film and television. In Australia he wrote for many medical, detective and comedy series and won the Best TV Script award. He was awarded a fellowship to the American Film Institute in Los Angeles, where he wrote the TV comedy *Alive and Kicking*. In the UK he is best known for originating many series including *Waiting for God* (BAFTA nominated), *Class Act, Trial by Marriage, The River, Life as We Know It, Truckies, Fear, Stress and Anger, Roy's Raiders, Honey for Tea* and *A Perfect State*. He was a core writer on *Midsomer Murders* and has written episodes of *The Last Detective, Murder in Suburbia, Stay Lucky* and *Moon and Son*. He has had three stage plays performed in Sydney, Hawaii and Jersey but only writes for theatre when he can afford it. He lives in Jersey and London, has two daughters and likes fishing in faraway places.

James Seabright presents *Waiting for God*; it began its UK Tour on 25 April 2017 in Eastbourne with the following cast and creatives:

TOM BALLARD	Jeffrey Holland
DIANA TRENT	Nichola McAuliffe
SARAH CHASE	Joanna Bending
GEOFFREY BALLARD	David Benson
DENNIS SPARROW	Peter Cadden
HARVEY BAINES	Samuel Collings
DOCTOR HENRY	Corinna Marlowe
JANE EDWARDS	Emily Pithon

Director	David Grindley
Designer	Jonathan Fensom
Lighting Designer	Jason Taylor
Sound Designer	Fergus O'Hare
Casting Director	Stephen Moore
Production Managers	Ben Arkell
	Patrick Malony
Company Stage Manager	Simon Bannister
Deputy Stage Manager	Julie Whitcombe
Acting Assistant Stage Manager	Anna Westlake
Costumer Supervisor	Emma Lindsay
Props Supervisor	Lizzie Frankl
Photography	Geraint Lewis
Touring Wardrobe Supervisor	Sara Markwick
Fight Director	Paul Benzing
Production Relighter	Adam Foley
Press Representation	Bright Media
Marketing, Advertising and Social Media	JHI
Graphic Design	Rebecca Pitt
General Management	Seabright Productions

CHARACTERS

DIANA TRENT An elderly but very feisty woman.
TOM BALLARD An elderly man. Whimsical. Lovely.
JANE EDWARDS (30s) Sad, flustered and lovesick.
HARVEY BAINES (30s) Vain and incompetent shyster.
SARAH CHASE/DOCTOR (30s) Diana's niece. Successful, charming. (Doubling as **DOCTOR** in Scene Eight)
GEOFFREY BALLARD/DOCTOR GYNO (40s) **TOM**'s son. A dull clod and multiple cuckold. (Understudies **DENNIS** and **HARVEY**)
DENNIS SPARROW A dithering vicar. (Understudies **TOM** and **GEOFFREY** and appears as **BASIL** in Scene Two)
DOCTOR JENNY HENRY/UNDERTAKER (Understudies **DIANA** and appears as **MILLY DAWKINS** in Scene Two)

Other understudies:
YOUNGER ACTRESS FOR JANE/SARAH/ DOCTOR HENRY (appears where required as a supernumerary)/ Acting ASM.

SETTING

One all-purpose set that doubles as verandah, apartments, hospital, church, doctor's room, fairground and Bournemouth seafront.

TIME

Running time approx 2 hrs 25 mins including one interval of 15 mins.

To Lucy and Daisy

ACT ONE

Scene One

The Bayview Retirement Home.

A verandah/conservatory.

Curtain up to reveal an all-purpose set designed to encompass various locations suggested more by lighting and furniture rather than traditional flats.

The conservatory/verandah is shared by two adjoining apartments. Each side of the conservatory has a set of outdoor furniture: a simple table and two chairs.

DIANA TRENT, *in her dressing gown, is sitting at her table playing a card game of solitaire.*

Fade music, bring up bird sounds. **DIANA** *sighs and mutters to herself as she turns over the cards.*

DIANA Oh for goodness sakes. Damn thing never comes out.

She glances round to see if she is being watched and then flicks a card over her shoulder. She is cheating at solitaire.

The bird song comes up a fraction. **DIANA** *looks up. Tuts.*

Oh do shut up. Damn birds. Tweet bloody tweet. All day long.

DIANA *calls to the next apartment.*

Henry! Hurry up with the crossword. My brain's turning to porridge over here... *(no response)* Henry, are you deaf? Oh yes... He is deaf.

She sighs and goes back to her cards.

JANE *(offstage)* Yoo hoo. Good morning.

DIANA Oh dear God. Not now, not Jane.

JANE EDWARDS, *the flustered, assistant manager of Bayview, enters.* **DIANA** *sighs and looks bleak as* **JANE** *bustles around tidying.*

JANE Good morning, Diana. Lovely day today.

DIANA It's cold and wet and they're forecasting a plague of frogs.

JANE But God gave you this day to enjoy.

DIANA Well bully for God. Did he also give me the brittle bones, the furred arteries, the irritable bowels and the flatulence that could rip out a palm tree?

JANE Um... I see you're not dressed yet.

DIANA So?

JANE *lifts her clipboard.*

JANE Well I was wondering if you'd...been.

DIANA Been?

JANE To the little room? To have your morning tinkle?

DIANA I beg your pardon.

JANE Harvey needs to know who's in the plastic sheet club as the laundry costs are a bit extra. I'll go and have a looksie, shall I? Check for damp bits.

As **JANE** *goes to straighten up* **DIANA** *hooks her round the neck with her walking stick. Squawk etc. and pulls her face down to hers.*

Diana!

DIANA You really are quite unspeakable.

JANE Please. You're hurting me.

DIANA Pah!

DIANA *lets her go.* **JANE** *straightens up and rubs her neck.*

JANE Oh goodness. Oh deary me. What on earth brought that on?

DIANA You haven't a clue, have you? Not a clue!

JANE I never have with you.

DIANA *shakes her head and sighs.*

DIANA I didn't mean to hurt you. I apologise.

JANE I forgive you.

DIANA Thank you.

JANE *does a bit more clearing up with sidelong glances at* **DIANA.**

JANE We're going on the big outing soon.

DIANA Oh hoo-bloody-ray. Harvey trying to kill us off again?

JANE Harvey is a very good man.

DIANA He's a bent little shyster who should be kebabbed from tonsils to Khyber Pass.

JANE That's very hurtful.

DIANA If you do it right.

JANE I happen to love Harvey very much.

DIANA Jane, he doesn't even like you touching him.

JANE Some men just find it difficult to express themselves on an emotional level.

DIANA Because they don't have an emotional level. Because they're smarmy little toads who live in the damp and fetid basement of the emotions.

JANE I'm not listening. We're going to Lourdes this year. Can I book you a seat on the minibus?

DIANA I don't do God. Or miracles. Or death by mini bus.

JANE A little faith might do you good.

DIANA Faith, Jane, is what helps you God-botherers make the quantum leap between the rational and the totally bloody ridiculous. I, on the other hand, am a sensible, clear-thinking atheist… Thank God.

JANE *turns to go but stops and looks out the window.*

JANE Oh… Um… I see your niece has left her car here. A Porsche.

DIANA Sarah lives in Chelsea so when she goes away she leaves her car here to stop the Russians stealing it.

JANE It's just that Harvey was a little worried you might actually try and drive it.

DIANA *had not thought of this before but the idea makes her look up and smile.*

DIANA Never crossed my mind.

JANE Sarah's so good the way she always comes and sees you.

DIANA Only because she's hoping that one day she'll find me dead as a parrot in a blender. She just wants my money.

JANE Harvey says persecution mania is very common amongst senior citizens.

DIANA Don't you call me a senior citizen.

JANE Well what are you then?

DIANA What do I look like?

JANE A senior citizen.

DIANA And when did I become a senior citizen?

JANE When you turned sixty of course.

DIANA Jane, on my sixtieth birthday I was hanging out of a helicopter on the Afghan borders, snapping various warlords as they tried to shoot my arse off.

JANE Goodness how colourful.

DIANA In decent cultures they don't have senior citizens. They have elders whom they respect and revere. Here they call us bed-blockers and leave us out in the snow to be eaten by wolves.

JANE Oh Diana. How did you get to be you?

DIANA Just lucky, I guess.

DIANA *goes back to playing solitaire.* **JANE** *watches her for a moment.*

JANE Do you enjoy playing with yourself?

DIANA Would you care to rephrase that?

JANE Would you like me to rustle up someone for you to play with?

DIANA No thank you. I like playing on my own. It's easier to cheat.

DIANA *chucks another card over her shoulder.*

And if I get bored I can always get old Henry to join me.

DIANA *peers at the next door apartment.* **JANE** *looks awkward.*

JANE Oh... You haven't heard?

DIANA Heard what?

JANE Henry has gone to a better place.

DIANA His sister's, in Devon?

JANE His father's, in heaven.

DIANA Oh...oh dear. What took him off then?

JANE He just sort of...stopped.

DIANA Terminal boredom. Poor old Henry. He was a nice fellow.

JANE Only here three months.

DIANA Yes... The turnover rate in that apartment is getting quite vulgar. Can hardly hear yourself talk for the thud of falling bodies.

JANE I thought you knew.

DIANA No. They keep these things quiet. Sometimes you see the hearses gliding through the hedgerows like circling sharks. But usually they just slip in under cover of darkness, then the sun comes up and everybody tries to ignore the untouched bowl of Frosties on the breakfast table.

JANE Oh Diana, you do depress me.

DIANA Oh, thank you.

JANE *(exiting)* I'll see you later.

DIANA One down. Who's next?

HARVEY *(offstage)* Here we are.

DIANA The idiot Baines. Oh goody.

HARVEY This is one of our premier apartments. Do have a look round, Mr Ballard.

HARVEY NIGEL BAINES *comes out of the other apartment and sees* **DIANA** *beaming at him. He stops.*

Oh... Diana.

DIANA Harvey. What a treat. Got a new boy already, have you? God, you don't want to nod off round here.

HARVEY No negative comments to the clients please. There are no rats here and I do not deal in used body parts.

He calls back inside.

And out here is your own private verandah-style conservatory.

GEOFFREY, TOM's *dull son, comes out of the apartment.*

See, lovely view, light and airy. I'm sure your father will love it here.

GEOFFREY Looks jolly nice. Doesn't it, Dad? Dad?

But Dad is not there. **GEOFFREY** *calls back inside.*

Dad. We're out here.

TOM *(offstage)* Coming. Just finishing some old cat food I found in the fridge.

HARVEY *looks alarmed.* **GEOFFREY** *laughs nervously.*

GEOFFREY Heheheh. My father's a bit of a joker. Who's that old dear?

GEOFFREY *indicates* **DIANA**, *who looks up, very aggrieved.*

HARVEY The verandahs are private but adjoining. That's your father's charming neighbour, Ms Trent.

GEOFFREY *edges across and shouts at* **DIANA**.

GEOFFREY Hello, dear. How are you?!

DIANA *shouts back even louder.*

DIANA I'm not bloody deaf. Nor am I simple. Jesus Christ!

DIANA *goes inside her apartment.*

GEOFFREY Crikey.

HARVEY *laughs nervously.*

HARVEY Good old Diana. Great sense of humour. We all love Diana. *(calls inside)* Mr Ballard.

GEOFFREY Dad.

There is a pause until **TOM***'s long leg arches out from behind a flat and he comes out doing an impersonation of a large bird. An emu. High stepping, elbows as wings with neck going back and forth and peering at everything. He wears a yellow waistcoat and bow tie. He struts downstage.*

HARVEY *looks to* **GEOFFREY**.

HARVEY What's he doing?

GEOFFREY Um... He's being...an emu.

HARVEY An emu, why?

GEOFFREY Emus like to carefully inspect their surroundings before nesting.

TOM *looks* **HARVEY** *up and down and round the back.*

HARVEY Er... There are clauses in the residency contract... incontinence...intellectual stability...

GEOFFREY He's fine... Dad, please. What do you think?

TOM *stops being an emu and looks out the window and opens his arms like a rock star opening his show.*

TOM Hellooooo, Bayview.

GEOFFREY Pretty good, eh?

TOM Wonderful, Geoffrey. Never seen anywhere so wonderful. It is the eighth wonder of the world... In fact it is so wonderful...

GEOFFREY If you don't like it you can come home.

TOM I don't think your wife would like that.

GEOFFREY Marion loves you, Dad. In her own way.

TOM She tried to bury me under the patio.

GEOFFREY She's just highly strung.

TOM And so she should be.

GEOFFREY Dad, I'm sorry it didn't work out but...

TOM It's okay Geoffy. You're just waving me off on another big adventure. I'll be fine.

GEOFFREY Are you sure?

TOM Yes really. It's okay. Te absolvo. See you in a few days.

GEOFFREY Oh...okay.

TOM Bye, Geoffy.

GEOFFREY *(exiting)* Bye.

TOM Lovely to have known you...son.

> **TOM** *waves goodbye and looks a bit sad then pulls himself together and turns back to* **HARVEY**.

> Poor boy. His wife is screaming mad.

> *But* **HARVEY**, *unhearing, is checking his clipboard and making notes.*

HARVEY Oh really, that's nice.

TOM Drinks like a fish.

HARVEY Jolly good.

TOM Shags like a rabbit.

HARVEY She sounds lovely. Okay, all done.

TOM So what's on today's agenda?

HARVEY Lunch in the dining room. Meet your new friends?

TOM I look forward to that.

HARVEY Great. I just know you're going to be really happy here, Ben.

TOM It's Tom.

> **HARVEY** *checks his notes.*

HARVEY You're absolutely right. Sharp as a tack, eh? Jolly good.

HARVEY *leaves.* **TOM** *emus around the verandah just as* **DIANA** *comes back out.*

TOM Hello.

DIANA *is wary. Nods and grunts.*

My name is Tom... Tom...Jones.

DIANA Oh yes.

TOM Yes. I sing songs and women throw their underwear at me. Sometimes with themselves still in it.

DIANA Oh holy crap. *(yells off)* Jane! Jane!

TOM It's alright. Just kidding. Bit of an ice-breaker. A conversational gambit. Banter, as they call it.

DIANA So you're not Tom Jones?

TOM No.

DIANA Good.

TOM I'm Sir Edmund Hillary.

DIANA Jane!

TOM No, no, I mean metaphorically. See I've arrived here at base camp today. About to set out on the next big adventure.

TOM *puts out a hand.*

Tom Ballard.

DIANA *looks at his hand.*

I don't bite.

DIANA I do. Diana Trent. *(They shake hands.)* Step into my office.

TOM So what brought you to this cosy little Sherpa's hut?

DIANA Arthritis and poverty. The favoured cocktail of the over-the-hill mob. Then a dodgy knee job a couple of years back...surgeon was probably very good with tractors...sold my fourth-floor flat and did a deal for life with this place. Fed, watered and buried. Hopefully in that order but I wouldn't count on it...

TOM You didn't have a husband?

DIANA Plenty, but none of them mine.

TOM Heheh. And before the timbers started creaking...?

DIANA Photo journalism. War zones mainly. Like Kate Adie; if you saw me when you were on holiday you knew you'd made a terrible mistake.

TOM *laughs.*

You travel much?

TOM Oh yes, every day I go off on my travels. Without moving an inch. I call it geographical meditation. Up the Amazon, trekking to the poles, down the corner shop... I've been everywhere, man.

DIANA Oh yes?

TOM And sometimes I visit great moments in history. Last week I was at the Battle of Hastings. Right in the thick of it. I said to King Harold, what's that?

He points up. **DIANA** *laughs.*

DIANA That's really terrible.

TOM I can see we're going to get on marvellously.

DIANA *(chuckling)* I can see I'm going to have to shoot myself.

JANE *comes out through* **TOM**'*s apartment.*

JANE Hello, Mr Ballard. I'm Jane Edwards, manage the care centre here. May I call you Ben?

TOM I'd prefer Tom.

JANE Really? And why's that?

TOM Oh you know, just a whim.

DIANA It's his name, you half-witted puddleduck.

JANE Oh, right… Tom. So we'll see you in the dining room for lunch, shall we?

TOM What's on the menu?

DIANA It's Thursday; chicken cholera. If I were you I'd wait for road-kill Friday. At least there's the element of surprise.

TOM I'm sure whatever it is it'll be wonderful.

JANE I'll put you and Diana at the same table.

JANE *exits.*

TOM Charming girl.

DIANA *tuts and puts her book aside.*

DIANA It's people like you who give the elderly a bad name, being sweet and dotty all over the place. You're an old fuddy-duddy. I, on the other hand, have still got my balls of steel.

DIANA *goes into her room.*

TOM Yes… I can hear them clanging together…like bells in the fog. Bong… Bong… Bong… Here is the six o'clock news.

TOM *reverts to emu and steps off, peering inside his apartment.*

Scene Two

Dining room.

DIANA *and* **TOM** *are sitting at a table in the dining room with* **BASIL** *and* **MILLY** *supping their soup to one side.*

TOM Not much of a turnout.

DIANA Bingo and booze day at the parish hall.

TOM So who are they?

DIANA That pile of cardigans is Milly Dawkins, who grows our dope supply, and the old scrotum opposite her is Basil the Bayview stud. We're mainly women here. All the other old men had heart attacks about ten days after they discovered Viagra.

TOM I was really lucky, I had a wonderful wife. Maggie. Slipped quietly away fifteen years ago now.

DIANA I am sorry. And that boring bloke was your son?

TOM Yes... Do you have children?

DIANA No... No, I haven't. Did you have a career?

TOM Oh yes. Financial whiz-kid, ruthless Wall Street bond trader, and finally money launderer to a Colombian drug cartel.

DIANA Accountant.

TOM Humble accountant, please. Forty years chained to the same desk in grovelling subservience.

DIANA Well we will have a lot in common.

TOM But I'm not as boring as I sound, you know.

DIANA That would be difficult.

TOM I got a very nice pension and a carriage clock.

DIANA Oh whoopee.

TOM Unfortunately my son's wife crushed the clock while shagging the chap who came to read the gas meter...

DIANA *gives him a quick look.*

...His name was Barney and he came from Wolverhampton. He was rather a nice fellow but we didn't see him again as my son switched power suppliers.

DIANA Does the phrase "too much information" have any resonance with you?

TOM *chuckles and sips his soup.*

TOM Eeergh.

TOM *doesn't like the soup.*

DIANA Nice soup, is it?

TOM In some cultures I believe they do drink their own urine. But not usually with mushrooms in it.

Maid delivers the next course.

And what is this meat?

DIANA *looks as* **TOM** *pokes with his fork.*

DIANA Labrador.

TOM And these carrots are out of a can. And the potatoes are soggy.

DIANA Yup.

TOM This is not what I'm paying for.

DIANA Welcome to the end of the rainbow, Dorothy.

HARVEY *comes in and starts his tour of the tables.*

TOM I'm going to have a serious word. I say...hello there. Mr Baines.

HARVEY *comes over.*

HARVEY Hi there, Ben. How's it going?

TOM This food is wretched.

HARVEY No one ever complains.

DIANA I complain every day.

HARVEY That's because complaining is your hobby, Diana.

TOM But why is it so...cheap?

HARVEY The catering budget is just that, Ben, a budget.

TOM So increase the budget.

HARVEY I just run the place. Budgets are decided by the board.

TOM And who are they?

HARVEY Professional people. Entrepreneurs, doctors, the better class of dentist.

TOM Tax dodgers. Might have guessed.

HARVEY Elderly care is a business which needs investors, who only put their money in if the returns are...you know...

TOM Obscene?

HARVEY I'd better get on.

But **TOM** *grabs* **HARVEY** *by the back of his jacket.*

TOM Stop right there.

HARVEY Ben, please. Armani.

TOM We are paying customers here, right. We pay; you provide a service. So what does that make you? Our employee. Right? So as your employ*er* I am going to give you instructions about the food.

HARVEY But I explained...

TOM From now on we will have fresh food served in an appetizing manner or I will call every newspaper and TV station for miles around and invite them all here for my gala event.

HARVEY And what will that be?

TOM *stands.*

TOM On the front steps of the Bayview Retirement Village I will publicly disembowel myself. Hara-kiri in front of the world media.

And **TOM** *gives a graphic mime show of disembowelling himself. With sound effects.*

Ugh...arrghh...ooh...errgh...flop splatter...blood and slippery bits all over the news in your area.

DIANA *has a good laugh and the others also applaud.* **TOM** *bows.*

HARVEY I try to do my best. I am a good man.

MILLY No you're not!

HARVEY *exits as they jeer at him.*

TOM So do I get the Diana Trent stamp of approval?

DIANA *looks at him for a beat.*

DIANA Show us your dick first.

TOM *laughs.*

Blackout.

Scene Three

Verandah.

A few weeks later. **TOM** *is sitting at his table in a yoga position with his eyes shut.*

DIANA *comes out of her place with an airgun, and fires a pellet out the window.*

DIANA Bloody pigeons. Tom, we have to find some way of stopping these buggers crapping on... Tom?

She has turned and found **TOM** *in his meditation position.*

Oh Lord. Where have you gone this time?

She goes and waves a hand in front of him.

Hello. Ground control to Major Tom.

No response. **DIANA** *tuts.*

Dull day here so he buggers off up the Amazon while I sit here gaping at the sodden countryside, wondering why life has become slower than a Leonard Cohen concert.

GEOFFREY *(offstage)* Helloooooo.

DIANA Oh God, Mr Excitement. Tom, wherever you are, stay there.

DIANA *grabs up a book and holds it in front of her face as* **GEOFFREY** *comes through from* **TOM***'s apartment.*

GEOFFREY Hello, Dad... Dad.

TOM *does not respond, keeps eyes closed.*

It's me, Dad. Geoffrey? Your son? Hello. I haven't got Marion with me.

TOM *smiles but switches it off rapidly as* **GEOFFREY** *turns to him.*

I've had Harvey on the phone. He doesn't think you're happy here.

No response. **GEOFFREY** *turns to* **DIANA.**

DIANA Your father isn't here at the moment.

GEOFFREY I think he is, Diana. I can see him.

DIANA He is on another plane.

GEOFFREY Oh really. He's gone off on a plane but left his body behind, eh? They'd love him at Ryanair. Flying without your body. They'd pack 'em in. Of course if you turned up with your body they'd probably charge extra and...

DIANA Geoffrey! Do we have to cut your head off to stop you blathering?

GEOFFREY Sorry, Diana.

DIANA So where's your deranged little wife today? We haven't seen her since she vomited over the geraniums.

GEOFFREY Marion has gone to Amsterdam.

DIANA To vomit over the tulips?

GEOFFREY Quite possibly.

DIANA Oh dear. Golf pro again?

GEOFFREY Not your business, Diana... Tennis coach.

DIANA God, she really does shag for the world eleven, doesn't she?

GEOFFREY Thank you for that. Where do you suppose Dad's "gone".

DIANA God knows. South Pole probably. Said he may be gone for some time.

GEOFFREY Is he alright?

DIANA Tickety-boo.

GEOFFREY It's just that Harvey said...

DIANA Harvey likes nice old people who take their drugs, shut up and don't eat too much. That is not your dad. He's an intellectual anarchist and he's fine, so you don't have to feel guilty today.

GEOFFREY Oh.

DIANA So off you go.

GEOFFREY You sure?

DIANA Yes.

GEOFFREY Okay... Bye, Dad. I hope it's nice wherever you are. Drop us a card eh?

GEOFFREY *laughs feebly and exits.*

DIANA God, what a waste of sperm.

DIANA *shoots.* **TOM** *watches.*

Come on, little birdies...come to Diana.

TOM That is one of the most blatantly malicious acts I have ever seen.

DIANA Oh, you're back.

TOM They're little birds, for God's sake.

DIANA I never hit them. I'm just trying to restructure their image of the elderly. Being unpleasant isn't just the prerogative of the young, you know.

She fires again.

So where have you been?

TOM Westminster. I was addressing the House on a matter of great importance. The injustice of ageing. I told them we had been cheated. We have worked hard all our lives and what happens to us?

DIANA Well in your case you go totally doolally.

TOM We get old. That's our reward for all our hard work.

DIANA So?

TOM Well it's all arse about, isn't it? If there was any real justice, we'd start old, then work our way back to being young.

DIANA And being babies again?

TOM No, no. God forbid. We'd stop getting younger at about twenty-three so that instead of farting about on SAGA cruises we would be doing loads of drugs and bonking ourselves into oblivion. Going out with a bang not a whimper. Literally. That would be justice.

DIANA *looks at him for a beat.*

DIANA You're either a great futurist thinker or a complete whack job.

TOM I like to assume the former but suspect the latter.

DIANA But I think we should put your idea into practice.

TOM How?

DIANA We should say we have just reached twenty-three and are now ready to rock.

TOM How do we do that?

DIANA *picks up the Porsche's car keys.*

DIANA The keys to my niece's Porsche.

TOM Wow. Can you drive?

DIANA Vaguely. Come on.

TOM Where will we go? St Tropez? Monte Carlo? Where are the movers and shakers hanging these days?

DIANA Bournemouth.

They exit.

JANE *enters.*

JANE *(calling into* **TOM***'s room)* Tom? Tom? I'm afraid the Lourdes trip has been cancelled. Harvey says that since we decided to leave Europe the French have deliberately pushed up their prices. Even if you don't get cured. So we're going to Stonehenge instead... Staying with Harvey's cousins. Lovely couple, druids... *(She sees he's not in.)* Oh... Tom?

Off we hear the roar of a Porsche starting up.

JANE *looks out as we hear the screech of tyres as the Porsche tears off down the drive.*

Oh my God... *(calls)* Harvey! Harvey!

JANE *scuttles out.*

Lights down.

Scene Four

The Bournemouth promenade.

MUSIC: "NO PARTICULAR PLACE TO GO".*

In the darkness we hear the screech of tyres as the car slides to a halt. Doors slam and gulls cry.

TOM *(offstage)* If we park here you'll get a ticket.

DIANA *(offstage)* My niece will get a ticket. Let's promenade.

They come on downstage looking out to sea.

That was exhilarating.

TOM Yes indeed. Nothing like a high-speed near-death experience to loosen the bowels of a summer's morn.

DIANA Glad to oblige.

TOM I once drove in the British Grand Prix, you know.

DIANA Of course you did.

TOM It was just before I landed on the moon.

DIANA One small step for mankind, one giant leap for Alzheimer's.

Gulls cry and they look up.

I love the gulls. Always moaning about something.

TOM They're departed souls trying to get the attention of the living.

DIANA And then dive-bombing them. My kind of bird.

TOM My parents would come down here during the Battle of Britain. They'd watch the little fighter planes duelling in the sky. Young lads way up there fighting for their lives. One of theirs went down and ragged cheer would ripple along the sea front...one of ours and all you could hear was the wind whispering farewell to a young soul joining the gulls.

DIANA *looks at him for a beat. He is a sensitive lad.*

DIANA Bollocks. Let's go to a movie.

TOM Don't you like to be beside the seaside?

DIANA No I don't. It's ghastly. Nothing more revolting than the English on a summer's day. A glimpse of sunshine and they unwrap their awful white, mildewed bodies and troll up and down vomit-strewn esplanades eating soggy chips and candy floss while their fat, ugly children stab each other.

TOM Diana...

DIANA And they don't enjoy it. They're really longing for the dark, dank autumn when they can crawl back onto their broken sofas, put their brains in neutral and spend the winter breaking wind in front of their God-awful soap operas.

TOM Dear Lord, Diana, you can't be so contemptuous of your fellow man.

DIANA Of course I can.

TOM But why bother?

DIANA Because if you're angry you know you're still alive.

TOM You really are a psychiatrist's holiday camp, aren't you?

DIANA Thank you.

TOM If you think life is one long bath in acid, why don't you pull the plug?

DIANA Suicide? No, no. There are too many people to get even with and the best way to do that is outlive them.

TOM But they'll be dead so won't witness your petty victories.

DIANA They might be watching from the afterlife.

TOM You don't believe in an afterlife.

DIANA I could be wrong. I'm not the Pope.

TOM Ah. So you're an agnostic. Not an atheist as claimed. You are open to being persuaded.

DIANA Oh no I'm not. I am impervious to any form of regimented belief system. I believe only in myself. And even there I have a few doubts. Come on. Let's go. Let's burn a little rubber.

DIANA *exits.*

TOM I didn't bring one with me.

TOM *exits.*

Lights down.

Scene Five

Conservatory. A little later.

SARAH *laying lunch.* **DIANA** *comes on, massaging her hip. In pain.*

DIANA Ow...ooooh...my bloody hip... Driving a Porsche round Bournemouth is about as hip-friendly as sliding down Everest in a bedpan.

SARAH *comes out carrying two plates of food.*

SARAH Serve you right. I left my car here for safekeeping, not so that you and your fancy man could go burning round the countryside like zonked-out teenagers. *(She grabs back her sunglasses from* **DIANA***'s head.)* And I'll have those back!

DIANA What's that?

SARAH What does it look like? It's lunch.

DIANA I'm not eating that.

SARAH Why not?

DIANA I can smell the cyanide from here or is it ground glass this time?

SARAH Both.

DIANA *pushes her plate away.*

This is pure unadulterated late-onset paranoia.

SARAH *swaps her and* **DIANA***'s plates and starts to eat that which was* **DIANA***'s.*

DIANA And I'm not falling for that one.

DIANA *pushes her new plate away.* **SARAH** *sighs and swaps them back again and takes a forkful off the other plate.*

You're waiting to get me with the pudding.

SARAH I am not trying to kill you. Much as I would like to sometimes, I'm actually trying to keep you alive.

DIANA Why?

SARAH God knows.

DIANA I'm not leaving you anything, you know.

SARAH You haven't got anything to leave.

DIANA Oh yes I have.

SARAH Not by my standards.

DIANA What does that mean?

SARAH How do you think I drive a Porsche and have a huge flat on the river?

DIANA You're a high-class tart.

SARAH I'm a banker. As well you know.

DIANA Tart would be preferable. At least then there might be some limit to the number of people you screwed.

SARAH Eat your cyanide and shut up.

DIANA *eats. Thinks.*

DIANA So why do you come here?

SARAH Seriously?

DIANA Yes.

SARAH Because you're family.

DIANA What does that mean?

SARAH Family is a tribal support system whereby people of the same blood look after each other. You and I are all we've got left in our family.

DIANA I was never a family person.

SARAH Yes you were. When I was a brat you were all over me. Presents after all your trips. Lots of hugs. Never forgot my birthday. You were lovely to me.

DIANA I don't remember that. Maybe it was some other aunt.

SARAH Oh God. I come here because I love you. Is that a concept totally beyond your fat-headed comprehension?

DIANA *looks at her.*

DIANA Well I don't want you coming here anymore.

SARAH Why on earth not?

DIANA I just don't.

SARAH You're being more perverse than usual today. Why?

DIANA Why do you think, girl? I want to stay in your memory as I was, when I was flying the world, living on my wits, when I was alive. When I was Diana Trent.

SARAH "Your autumn years are the best years." You said that.

DIANA I was lying. The young booze and sex years are the best years. Autumn years are rubbish. I'm just a clapped-out wreck and I don't want you to remember me like this. Falling to pieces. Can't you see? I'm ashamed of this...me... ashamed...

SARAH That's so silly.

DIANA Not from here it isn't. Now I have to rest. Goodbye, Sarah.

DIANA *goes to her door. She stops and turns.*

Sorry.

SARAH See you next month, Aunty.

DIANA Aunt!

DIANA *exits.* **SARAH** *sighs. There is a crashing sound from off.*

(offstage) Ow!

SARAH Diana. Are you alright?

DIANA *(offstage)* Fuck fuck fuckity fuck fuck.

Blackout.

Scene Six

Hospital room.

A few hours later. **DIANA***'s bed has now converted to her hospital bed and sits centre stage with a suggestion of hospital paraphernalia round it.*

SARAH *and* **JANE** *are sitting either side of the bed on which* **TOM** *is lying, fully clothed.*

JANE So how did it happen?

SARAH Lost her balance, fell heavily. They've given her a new hip.

TOM And hopefully vented her spleen at the same time.

HARVEY *comes in.* **JANE** *gets up and gives him her seat.*

HARVEY Hello, sorry I'm late. So Diana, eh? How is she? Oh God, her bed's empty. How tragic. I'm so sorry. I didn't know. It must have been so quick. Well that's probably a blessing, eh?

JANE She's in physio, Harvey.

She touches **HARVEY**.

HARVEY Jane, you're touching me.

JANE Sorry, Harvey.

HARVEY So physio, eh? Well what a relief. Wonderful. But I guess she'll never walk again and have to leave Bayview. So sad.

TOM Harvey, how did you qualify for your job?

HARVEY I trained for over three weeks, Tom.

TOM And they didn't tell you that after a hip operation you are usually more mobile than you were before the op.

HARVEY Really?

TOM She's taking up kick-boxing next week.

HARVEY Oh...great...how wonderful. Come along, Jane.

HARVEY *walks out with* **JANE** *scuttling after him.*

(offstage) Diana, how lovely to see you, so glad you're going to be... Ow! Do you have to hit me every time we meet?

DIANA *shuffles in on a frame. They get up to help her.*

SARAH Let me help.

DIANA I'm quite capable. What are you doing back here?

TOM How are you feeling today?

DIANA Fed up. Didn't want a new hip.

SARAH You'd probably have needed a new one soon anyway. At your age.

They help **DIANA** *climb back into bed.*

DIANA At my age? At my age? You sound like a doctor. A male doctor. They're useless for women. When you're a girl it's "Everything will be fine when your periods start", then it's "You'll be fine when you've had a baby" then it's "The change will fix you". And now it's "Well you've got to accept these things at your age". When is there a stage in a woman's life when she is cured of her ills without going through some male-defined age barrier? Eh?

She has her face into **TOM***'s.*

TOM I don't know, I'm a bloke.

DIANA When she's dead. Unless she's a Buddhist, then they'll say "Not to worry, things will be better in your next life". What's the matter?

SARAH I want to talk to you. Important.

DIANA Tom, you need a pee...

TOM Righto. I'll alert the fire brigade.

TOM *exits.*

DIANA So what's up?

SARAH Diana, what do you think of marriage?

DIANA Marriage? Dreadful bourgeois feudal bollocks aimed at tying women to the sink and reducing them to chattels.

SARAH Uhuh... And what do you think of Dick?

DIANA Haven't had any for years.

SARAH Richard! My fella. Last night he asked me to marry him. What do you think?

DIANA Well Dick is charming, good-looking, smart and being investigated by the serious fraud squad. Why do you have to get married?

SARAH Because he's asked me.

DIANA Harvey Baines asked me to be a suicide bomber. Doesn't mean I have to say yes... All that sex and passion soon burns out, you know. Then marriage is just years and years of dull routine, average sex, compromise, despair, depression, futility and, only if you're really lucky, the blessed release of an early death.

SARAH How do you know? You never tried it.

DIANA No, because the men I fell for were always pirates, swashbucklers, hooligans... I wouldn't have marry them in fit but the decent ones, the good guys...they bored me silly.

SARAH Dick's a pirate.

DIANA And I... I am here. Solo. On me tod.

SARAH So what do I do?

DIANA Dive in, I suppose, and the first time he steps out of line you string him up by the offending parts. Meanwhile give him everything you've got and if you're not gloriously happy...just strangle the little sod.

SARAH Thank you, Diana.

DIANA Is that what you wanted to hear?

SARAH Of course. Should we get married down here?

DIANA Could be tricky. Dennis Sparrow, our wonderful vicar, lost the plot years ago. He'd probably bury you.

SARAH We're in a bit of a hurry.

DIANA Oh... Up the duff, are we?

SARAH Just a bit. I think.

DIANA Clever girl. Always test the product before you buy.

SARAH Love you!

DIANA Get off...

They hug.

Lights down.

Scene Seven

Dining room.

TOM, *in black suit, is sat at his dining table. He is reading his paper but he doesn't feel well. Indigestion?*

He lays his paper down and loosens his collar then leans back in his chair breathing hard and wincing.

HARVEY *and* **JANE** *come in, both in dark funeral clothes. They are carrying a few bunches of flowers.* **HARVEY** *hands his to* **JANE.**

HARVEY Right, spread them around the room Jane. Show that I really care when one of our dear residents falls off his perch.

JANE I'm not sure this is right, Harvey.

HARVEY Jane, flowers are flowers. It's not like they're going to do any good sitting outside the crematorium. Hello, Tom, you're a bit early for lunch.

TOM *just grunts and breathes. Obviously ill.* **JANE** *arranges some flowers in a vase on* **TOM***'s table.*

JANE There we go. I'm sure Basil would have liked you to have these.

She puts a large vase of lilies in front of **TOM** *so that we can't see his suffering so much. He groans.*

TOM Aaaah.

JANE Aww. It was a very nice funeral.

HARVEY Rev. Dennis thought it was a wedding.

JANE Made it a bit more cheerful. I love weddings. *(She lalas the wedding march.)*

LA DA DEH DA DA...

DIANA *comes in on her stick, also in black. Hits* **JANE** *lightly.*

DIANA Do be quiet, Jane.

HARVEY Diana, enjoy the funeral, did we?

DIANA Don't be an arse, Harvey.

HARVEY Such a shame you couldn't make the Stonehenge trip. It was a beautiful day, sun shining, birds singing.

DIANA Basil dying.

HARVEY He'd had a good run.

JANE And now he's gone to his maker.

DIANA He died because he fell out the back of your clapped-out minibus.

HARVEY His heart gave out.

DIANA Because he was bouncing along a dual carriageway.

HARVEY You're always so negative.

DIANA And what are these things doing on our table? You know I'm allergic to flowers.

She picks up the lilies to reveal **TOM** *now looking worse.*

Tom? What are you doing?

TOM I think I'm dying.

DIANA I'll do the black jokes, thank you.

TOM No, seriously. I'm...oh dear.

TOM *slumps forward.*

DIANA Oh Jesus. Call an ambulance.

HARVEY Let's not be hasty here. Ambulances are bad for business.

DIANA What?

HARVEY We've got the minibus.

DIANA *hits* **HARVEY** *in the balls.*

JANE Oh, Harvey!

DIANA Jane, get a bloody ambulance. Come on, Tom.

DIANA *loosens* **TOM***'s tie.* **JANE** *dials her phone.*

TOM Oh dear...feel a bit...oh God...

He shuts his eyes and slumps to one side.

DIANA Tom... Tom, stay with us. Jane!

JANE Could we have an ambulance please? Bayview Retirement Village.

HARVEY Jane, what are you doing?

JANE *(into phone)* ...Suspected heart attack.

HARVEY I haven't had a heart attack. Jane, I said no ambulance.

DIANA *knocks him down again.*

DIANA Tom... Tom... You're going to be fine... Just fine...fine...

Fade down as **DIANA** *gently pats* **TOM***'s face.*

Lights down. Sound of ambulance up.

Scene Eight

Hospital.

DIANA *waits anxiously in the hospital corridor with* **JANE.**

DIANA This is all it is now. A life made up of endless hospital visits.

JANE At least Harvey's going to be alright.

DIANA Then one day, it's your turn. You come in, conk out and they bag you up, bung you out the back and you're down the crem for the final barby.

JANE His testicles are the size of bowling balls. You really must stop hitting him.

DIANA It's only the persecution of crass, venal idiots like Harvey Baines that keeps me going.

JANE I'm going to collect him from downstairs. I'm sure Tom will be fine.

JANE *toddles off.* **DIANA** *looks up to the heavens.*

DIANA God. I don't believe in you and you probably have severe doubts about me. But if there is a scintilla of a possibility that I could be wrong, however unlikely, and you actually have some influence over life and death, would you kindly pull your celestial digit out of your holy arse and get Tom through this in one piece.

A **YOUNG FEMALE DOCTOR** *(double with* **SARAH***) comes out of a door.* **DIANA** *intercepts her.*

How is he? Tom Ballard?

DOCTOR Are you the wife?

DIANA No, I'm not the wife.

DOCTOR Well I'm sorry. I can only divulge information to the wife.

The **DOCTOR** *walks away.* **DIANA** *yells after her.*

DIANA Then I hope you've got a bloody shovel 'cos she's been dead for fifteen years. Are there any human beings in this place?

But the **DOCTOR** *has gone.* **DIANA** *sits again. Sighs.*

Oh come on, Tom. Not you. Not yet. In this dreary, anodyne world the relentlessly daft must be allowed to survive.

GEOFFREY *comes round the corner.*

GEOFFREY Well that's a relief. He's going to be fine. Just a minor occlusion.

DIANA How do you know that?

GEOFFREY The doctor just told me.

DIANA She told you.

GEOFFREY Yes. Dad's going to be fine.

DIANA Oh...good.

GEOFFREY But I think he better come back home for a bit.

DIANA And how does Marion feel about that?

GEOFFREY I took your advice, Diana. Told her to shut the eff up and behave herself.

DIANA Well done, Geoffrey. That's wonderful. See, I told you, sometimes you just have to stand up to people in this life and they respect and love you for it.

GEOFFREY She's moved in with our accountant.

GEOFFREY *just looks at her.* **DIANA** *looks a bit awkward.*

DIANA Oh...well... Maybe he'll get you a good rebate.

GEOFFREY He was also my best man.

DIANA Oh, Geoffrey, I am sorry. I wish I gave a damn but I just don't.

The door opens and **TOM** *comes out in his hospital gown. They go to prop him up.*

Tom.

GEOFFREY Dad.

DIANA You're alright?

TOM I think so. Unless of course I've died and gone to heaven, in which case I'm a little disappointed with the preponderance of magnolia?

GEOFFREY Dad. You're not dead.

DIANA You're fine. Just a bit of a turn.

GEOFFREY I'm going to take you home.

TOM To Bayview?

GEOFFREY No...home with me.

TOM No thanks, Geoffy. Home is where the heart is and I believe I lost mine at Bayview. Probably down the back of the sofa.

TOM *puts an arm round* **DIANA***'s shoulder.*

Hello, old thing.

They smile at each other.

GEOFFREY I'll get the car.

GEOFFREY *exits.*

TOM Let's go then.

DIANA Are you sure you should be leaving without being properly discharged?

TOM God, Diana. Do you never listen to your own lectures? To stay alive you have to be bloody-minded and contrary at all times.

DIANA I was just theorising.

TOM Well I'm not. I have just felt the clammy fingers of something dark seeking me out. I have to get out of here and into the sunlight before it catches me.

TOM *turns upstage baring his buttocks through the back of his gown.*

DIANA I clobbered Harvey.

TOM Atta girl.

DIANA *links his arm and helps him off.* **JANE** *comes on, calling back.*

JANE Come along, Harvey. We haven't got all day.

HARVEY *(offstage)* I can hardly walk, Jane. What am I going to do?

JANE You'll be fine, Harvey. Use both hands.

HARVEY *comes on clutching a bag of ice to his balls and walks slowly across stage.*

Scene Nine

Conservatory.

A few months later. **TOM** *is knitting a long, twisted, knitted tube with kinks in it.*

TOM Knit one, pearl one, knit one, pearl one. I don't even know what that means.

JANE *comes bustling in.*

JANE Hello, Tom, what are you knitting?

TOM They are booties. For Sarah's baby.

JANE Oh... Is she having a giraffe with rickets then? Where is Diana?

TOM In a terrible state. Running round in a flat panic.

JANE Doesn't sound like her.

DIANA *comes out.*

DIANA What's the time?

TOM Now?

DIANA No, in a parallel universe. Of course now.

TOM It's one hour closer than it was an hour ago when you last asked. There's still two days to go.

DIANA I have to go to New York for a week.

TOM Diana, have some gin.

He pours gin into a mug.

JANE Isn't it exciting? A new baby.

DIANA *is looking out the window.*

DIANA Oh my God – what's that great lump waddling up the path?

TOM *looks out.*

TOM It's the lovely Sarah herself.

TOM *goes out the door.*

JANE I'll make some tea.

JANE *scuttles off.*

DIANA I can't do this. I can't be here.

TOM *comes back in with* **SARAH**.

SARAH Hello, Aunty.

TOM Here you go. Sit there.

DIANA Are you alright?

SARAH Fine.

DIANA You look like a beached whale. Do you want us to tow you back out to your pod?

SARAH Do tell her to shut up.

TOM Diana. Shut up.

DIANA Why do you have to have it down here?

SARAH Because since my husband went to jail I need you to help me out.

DIANA The hospitals down here are feudal.

SARAH They're fine. I've checked. What on earth is this?

SARAH *has spotted* **TOM**'*s bootie and picks it up.* **TOM** *snatches it back.*

TOM It's a donkey's willy warmer. I'll get some more tonic.

TOM *exits.*

SARAH I'm doing natural childbirth...special breathing and all that. I'll give you a crash course.

DIANA Sarah, just hang on a minute.

SARAH What's the matter?

DIANA I can't be there.

SARAH What?

DIANA I can't be there. At the birth.

SARAH I don't understand. Why not?

DIANA I'm...I'm squeamish.

SARAH Diana, you were a war correspondent...you've seen more blood and gore than...

DIANA Alright then, it's babies...breeding...and the whole concept of the continuation of the species in a ghastly, godforsaken, rotten, dismal, manky old world.

SARAH Well, that's encouraging.

DIANA I can't be part of it. Sorry.

SARAH And the real reason?

DIANA What do you mean?

SARAH The truth, Diana... Try the truth.

DIANA *wanders around, shakes her head.*

DIANA I never had any children...

SARAH Because you didn't want any. You weren't the mummy type.

DIANA Yes...that's what I said. Yelled from the rooftops so loud I believed it myself. But that wasn't the truth.

SARAH Go on.

DIANA I couldn't have children. I did try but there was something twisted or knotted inside me. In more ways than one probably.

SARAH Diana...

DIANA I don't mean I'm unfulfilled as a woman or anything so claptrap cretinous. Far from it. It's just, I mean, look at all the people who do breed. Everyone. God, even Harvey Baines could probably manage it with a manual and a following wind. But I couldn't. I couldn't join the most inexclusive club in the world so I'm sorry, I can't. I just can't.

SARAH *puts a hand on her arm.*

SARAH You do talk crap sometimes.

DIANA I find it helps.

SARAH Since Mum died, I've always looked to you.

DIANA Well you shouldn't. Your mother was an orchid. Rare and wonderful. But I'm not. I'm a crabby old cactus. I can't take her place.

SARAH You really do live in mortal fear of being loved, don't you?

DIANA *turns away.* **SARAH** *looks at her for a second then suddenly gets up and gasps and grabs the table and has a contraction. Blowing noises.*

Phoo...phooo...

She staggers. **TOM** *comes in. They both look on. Puzzled.*

DIANA What is she doing?

TOM Damned if I know.

SARAH I'm having a baby!

TOM Oh wonderful...more hot water and plenty of it.

SARAH This isn't a film.

DIANA No, no, you can't be. It's not until Wednesday. It's in my diary. Look. The third.

SARAH Aaaaarrrrrrrgh!

DIANA Oh Jesus, Tom, call an ambulance, no, call a doctor, no, call the hospital. I'm leaving.

SARAH *grabs* **DIANA***'s arm.*

SARAH Diana! My mother isn't here. My husband isn't here. I'm scared. I need you. Please help me.

DIANA *looks anguished.*

DIANA Oh... Bugger.

DIANA *and* **TOM** *help* **SARAH** *exit into* **TOM***'s apartment.* **JANE** *enters with a tray of tea.*

JANE Here we are. Nice cup of tea.

Blackout.

In the blackout we hear an ambulance siren followed by doors slamming, people calling, the rattle of a hospital trolley. **SARAH** *yelling through her contractions.*

Scene Ten

Delivery room. Daytime.

The birth takes place behind a black gauze. **DIANA** *at the head of the bed helping* **SARAH** *with the breathing and pushing.*

DOCTOR GYNO *(***GEOFFREY** *doubling) down the business end.*

DIANA And one, two, three...puuuuuuuuuuuuuush!

SARAH Aaaaaaaaaargh!

DR GYNO Keep going. Keep going.

SARAH Aaaaaaaaaargh!

DIANA Come on, harder or we'll be here all night. Puuuuuuuush!

Again they strain together...then the contraction stops and **SARAH** *flops.*

Why have you stopped?

SARAH The contraction has passed.

DR GYNO *proffers an oxygen mask.*

DR GYNO Do you want some oxygen?

DIANA Thank you.

DIANA *snatches the mask and has a quick inhale. They all look at her.*

Oh...sorry.

SARAH How many more?

DR GYNO Next one should do it.

DIANA I should have had the epidural.

SARAH Aaaarrrggh.

DR GYNO Here it comes!

DIANA Okay...one, two, three... Puuuuuush!

And **SARAH** *and* **DIANA** *strain and gasp together.*

DR GYNO Here we come...one more.

DIANA Push.

SARAH Aaaaaaaaaaaaaargh!

DR GYNO That's it...out we come.

Sound effects: baby howling.

DIANA Oh my God.

SARAH What is it?

DIANA My God...it's a rabbit...no it isn't, it's a boy with an enormous... What the hell's that?

DR GYNO The umbilical cord!

DIANA So what is it?

DR GYNO It's a little girl.

DIANA My God...it is...it's a girl... I've had a little girl... I've had a little girl.

SARAH Congratulations!

DIANA *breaks down in tears.*

DIANA I can't bear it!

SARAH It's all right, Diana, it's alright. All over now.

SARAH *proffers the baby to* **DIANA**.

DIANA May I? Oh thank you, thank you, thank you.

DIANA, *sobbing and laughing, comes downstage into her own spotlight with the wrapped baby and as she cries and sobs and repeats over and over.*

I did it. I did it. I did it.

We gradually fade to black.

Curtain.

Interval

ACT TWO

Scene One

TOM's bedroom.

A few months later. TOM, *sipping a cup of tea, is sitting in his dressing gown in a chair by the bed while* DIANA *sleeps, bare shouldered, in the bed. She is smiling in her sleep.*

JANE *comes in and starts bustling around not noticing* DIANA *as she opens the curtains.*

JANE Good morning, Tom.

TOM Morning, Jane.

JANE What a party last night. It's the same every birthday. Singing, dancing, dentures in the fish tank. And God knows where Diana is. Her bed's not been slept in. I'm worried something might have happened to her.

TOM Er... Jane.

TOM *points to* DIANA *asleep in his bed.*

JANE Oh there she is. Thank goodness. I thought she might be in jail again.

JANE *goes back to collecting the empty bottles. Then freezes as she realises what she has seen. She turns and goes back and looks down at* DIANA *and then at* TOM.

She's in your bed.

TOM Yes, Jane.

JANE She's smiling in her sleep.

TOM Yes, Jane.

JANE Oh dear Lord.

JANE *rushes out.*

TOM *chuckles then takes a long, deliberately noisy slurp of his tea.*

DIANA*'s eyes open. Staring ahead.*

DIANA Where am I? Am I dead?

TOM Far from it.

DIANA Tom?

TOM That's me.

DIANA What are you doing in my room?

TOM You're in my room.

DIANA What?

TOM In my bed. Buon giorno.

DIANA *looks round the room, then at* **TOM***...then she slowly lifts the covers a fraction and looks down the bed.*

DIANA Ah!

She shuts the covers down quickly.

TOM Want a cup of tea?

DIANA Don't change the subject.

TOM *just grins and sips his tea.* **DIANA** *looks under the sheets again.*

Where are my knickers?

TOM On top of the wardrobe.

DIANA How could you? How could you?

TOM I didn't.

DIANA You promise?

TOM Well I'm not sure. It depends if you are referring to what I'm referring. Or not.

DIANA No I am not. I'm sure I'm not. We always talk at cross-purposes. I must have been talking about something else.

TOM Oh well I didn't do something else.

DIANA Other than what?

TOM I don't know. I'm losing track here.

DIANA Tom!

TOM Yes, Diana?

DIANA Whatever we did...whatever I'm doing here...we didn't make love, did we?

TOM Oh yes, we did that.

DIANA Oh my God!

TOM Is there some kind of a problem?

DIANA Well of course there is. There's me. And you. And sex. My God, you took advantage of me.

TOM Did I?

DIANA You are a total and utter swine.

TOM That's a bit strong.

DIANA A woman takes refuge in your room, goes to sleep in your bed and you come in and...take her...use her. You should be in jail.

TOM Diana.

DIANA This is the end of everything, Tom.

TOM Diana.

DIANA You were my friend. I trusted you. How could you do it?

TOM Well not without a bit of help actually.

DIANA What?

TOM It was your idea, Diana. After the party we came back here and had some more gin, you told me about your one-night stand with Keith Richards and I told you about my marriage to Jane Fonda, then you passed out on my bed.

DIANA And then you...

TOM I went to sleep in the chair there. Then about 3am you shook me awake and gave me a long carpe diem lecture. "We only have a few good times in this life and we must grab them with both hands" ...And so you did.

DIANA Oh my God.

TOM My eyeballs nearly bounced off the walls. I really didn't take advantage of you, Diana.

DIANA No, no, I know you didn't. That was my early feminist speech. Whenever I fancied a man and didn't have time for all the fiddle-faddle, I'd bang on about how women should carpe any diem they damn well pleased. As soon as they said "When?" Well...basket cases by breakfast time.

TOM Yes I think I popped a few rivets myself.

DIANA I am sorry, Tom.

TOM Why?

DIANA Well, you know...your wife, Maggie. I know how faithful you are to her memory.

TOM It's been fifteen years since she died. Besides, Maggie liked a good laugh.

DIANA I beg your pardon?

TOM I mean she had a big heart.

DIANA So have you, Tom. A very big heart.

TOM Yes well...goes with the rest of me, eh?

DIANA Don't be puerile! Keep it in proportion. You did your bit. I did my bit. It wasn't Gone with the bloody Wind.

TOM Absolutely. Keep it in proportion.

DIANA And forget it ever happened.

TOM Oh definitely. Never happened. All forgotten... Can we do it again?

DIANA No!

TOM Why not?

DIANA You have a weak heart.

TOM If you've gotta go...

DIANA No. No, no... I'm not having that happen. Not again. Last time took down a Tory government.

TOM But it was such fun. It showed we were still alive. Shaggo ergo sum.

DIANA Yes, yes, thank you.

TOM And Harvey Baines would hate it. The thought of old people having fun could kill him.

DIANA Well...maybe on saints' days.

TOM Fine. Saints' days it is. What's the date?

DIANA Seventeenth?

TOM Isn't that the feast of St Kermit and All Frogs?

DIANA Get out of here.

Blackout.

Scene Two

Conservatory.

A few days later. **JANE** *is delivering newspapers and talking to herself.*

JANE Oh Diana...how could you? How could you? Maybe I should drink more.

HARVEY *comes in with an application form.*

HARVEY Jane. Jane. Jane, the golf club have turned down my membership application. I don't understand. What's wrong with it?

JANE *takes the application form and reads off it.*

JANE "Name: Harvey Nigel Baines. Education: Some. What's your current handicap? ...I'm too sexy for my shirt?"

HARVEY Banter, Jane. Show them I'd be a fun guy in the bar. Told them I'd learn the golf stuff later but they still turned me down. Why?

JANE I expect it was fear, Harvey. Terrified of what would happen if a man of your obvious charisma were let loose amongst their wives.

HARVEY Yes...right. Hadn't thought of that.

JANE Maybe if you were sort of...like...kind of...married they'd feel safer.

HARVEY Good point, Jane.

HARVEY *heads for the door then stops, turns and thinks... going through the pros and cons. Then looking at* **JANE**.

Jane...would you like to have dinner tonight?

JANE That would be very nice, Harvey.

HARVEY Good. See you later then. God, I'm clever.

HARVEY *exits.* **JANE** *does a little manic dance on the spot.*

Offstage we hear **TOM***'s loo flush.*

DIANA *comes out, listening to the flushing.*

DIANA God, bloody plumbing in this place. Jane, Tom's lavatory is on the blink. Keeps flushing itself.

JANE *doesn't respond.*

Jane...? Jane? Jane, have you gone deaf?

JANE I'm sorry, Diana, I just don't feel I can talk to you anymore.

DIANA Well that's a bonus, but why?

JANE I think you know why.

DIANA Oh God, Jane. Sit down.

JANE I'd rather not, thank you.

DIANA Jane, sit down or I'll chop your legs off and nail the stumps to the chair.

JANE *sits hastily.* **TOM***'s loo flushes again.* **DIANA** *notes this.*

Now what's the matter with you? Are you put out because Tom and I are making the beast with two backs?

JANE Oh please.

DIANA Knotting and gendering like toads in a cistern?

JANE That's disgusting.

DIANA That's Shakespeare.

JANE Well he's disgusting too then.

DIANA *sighs.*

DIANA How do you see me, Jane?

JANE You're the Boadicea of Bayview, someone they all look up to and respect... But now...now you've done...this...

DIANA Oh, Jane, you dismal, twisted dimwit… Where have you been for the last umpteen years? Has every single tenet of current thinking passed you by on the other side? Have you been so totally brainwashed by the constant drip of kiddy TV that you believe that sex only takes place between beautiful young people who jump in and out of each other's jeans.

JANE But you, Diana.

DIANA What's wrong with me?

JANE You're a pensioner.

DIANA I'm a woman! It's people like you with your stereotypical ideas who've made me feel old. But I'm not. And now, thanks to a bit of cheap plonk, a new hip, some WD40 and a fully functioning Tom Ballard, I have re-discovered the fact that I am still a total woman firing on all cylinders and perfectly capable of going off like the proverbial rocket.

JANE Well I suppose if it's medicinal…and makes you feel better…

DIANA It does. A million times better. In fact we should all be having sex round here.

JANE But shouldn't you be a bit fitter? I mean you could hurt yourselves.

DIANA Nonsense. Just 'cos we no longer do it tearing along country lanes in the back of a mini with one foot out the window and the other over the driver's shoulder… God that was fun…doesn't mean we can't still be at it. We just have to take it easy and try not to fall over our Zimmer frames.

JANE Golly…

DIANA And we must totally obliterate the idea that sex amongst the elderly is something tacky or furtive.

JANE You're right, Diana.

DIANA I am on a mission.

JANE So what do we do?

DIANA First step, tell the idiot Baines we need twenty-four-hour lighting so that we can do corridor creeping without getting lost all the time.

JANE Yes, Diana. Great.

DIANA And a condom vending machine in reception.

JANE Oh I don't think there's much fear of pregnancy.

DIANA Jane, condoms aren't just for preventing pregnancies. Some people like to pull them over their heads and rob banks. *(loo flushes)* Call maintenance and get that thing fixed.

JANE Oh there's nothing wrong with the facilities. It's just Tom. He keeps going all the time.

DIANA What?

JANE He says he keeps feeling like tinkling all the time but when he gets there...no tinkle tinkles.

DIANA And this means nothing to you?

JANE Should it?

DIANA *heads for* **TOM***'s door...*

DIANA Tom, get your coat, we're going to the quacks. *(back to* **JANE***)*

DIANA *opens her mouth to say something but can't. Just wags her finger at* **JANE** *in exasperation and exits.*

Lights down.

Scene Three

DOCTOR'*s surgery.*

Some days later. **TOM** *is behind a curtain with* **DR HENRY. DIANA** *is waiting with* **GEOFFREY**.

DIANA He had a blockage. In his waterworks.

GEOFFREY Yes, Diana.

DIANA They had to drain him.

GEOFFREY Yes Diana.

DIANA They ran a tube straight up his whatsit.

GEOFFREY Yes, thank you, Diana. I do know the procedure. Once after Marion had been to Morocco with our plumber I had to...oh never mind.

TOM *comes out from behind the curtain as* **DR HENRY** *washes up.*

TOM What ho. Here we are again.

GEOFFREY You okay, Dad?

TOM Oh yes. Great fun. Rubber glove and a bit of lubricant. Like being back at school.

DR HENRY *enters from behind the curtain absently jotting notes.*

DIANA So what's wrong with him?

The **DOC** *ignores* **DIANA** *and keeps making notes.*

DR HENRY Right, Mr Ballard, what we have here is a classic problem. Our prostate is a bit swollen, I'm afraid.

DIANA And why is our prostate swollen?

TOM Diana, it is my prostate. Not ours.

The **DOC** *scribbles more notes.* **DIANA** *snatches her pad from her.*

DIANA Hello? If you could just finish your novel later we would like to know what's wrong with us.

DR HENRY What do you know about the prostate gland?

TOM I know it's kept in a very silly place.

DR HENRY With age all our mechanisms get stiffer and produce more fibrous tissue, in the case of the prostate this process causes it to swell and block off the urethra. You know what the urethra is?

TOM Oh yes... Urethra Franklin, wonderful singer.

DIANA Is it cancerous?

DR HENRY That's a very emotive word.

DIANA It certainly is. So will he see a few more summers or should we just leave him by the bins on the way out?

DR HENRY We need to do a few more tests.

GEOFFREY Come on, Dad.

GEOFFREY *and* **TOM** *head for the exit.* **DIANA** *looks up to God.*

DIANA Don't you do this. Don't you bloody dare.

Lights down.

Scene Four

Conservatory.

MUSIC: "SECOND TIME AROUND".

DIANA *is clicking away on her laptop. The baby is in a crib next to her.*

DIANA When you reach a certain age there's one sentence that makes your blood run cold: "We need to do a few more tests". Google "prostate problems". Wow. Seventeen million results in point two of a second. I'm sorry but I don't function that fast so just slow down, stop showing off and let me know if the old bugger's going to be okay. Okay?

The baby starts to make whimpering noises. DIANA *rocks the crib.*

Oh sorry. Are you alright, short person? I do wish she'd give you a name.

Baby gurgles.

You sound like a little lavatory, don't you? You want me to tell you a story? Cinderella. Silly girl who fell for a prat who could only remember her shoe size. The end.

SARAH *appears in the doorway, unseen by* DIANA. *She watches on as* DIANA *leans in and tickles the baby.*

You do know you're very beautiful... You're the only beautiful thing left in the world...

She looks up and sees SARAH *in the doorway. Snaps back to usual* DIANA.

Ugly little bruiser, isn't she?

SARAH They all are.

DIANA She's grown.

SARAH They're supposed to. They're not bonsai.

SARAH *starts to gather up the baby stuff.*

DIANA She breaks my heart.

SARAH Goodness, an outburst of human feeling.

DIANA I can feel. I can feel.

SARAH Really? Through all that cynicism.

DIANA Cynicism is the romantic's condom. It protects them from the awfulness of life.

SARAH Cheery as ever.

DIANA Sorry. So how was prison? How's Dick?

SARAH He's running a Ponzi scam on D wing.

DIANA Good man.

SARAH When does Tom get his results?

DIANA Today. He should have them by now but he hasn't phoned so I don't know whether he's going to live or die. He's so selfish I could kill him.

SARAH Well let me know as soon as you hear.

DIANA Of course. Have you got a name for the baby yet? I can't keep calling her "short person".

SARAH Yes. I'm going to call her Diana. After her great aunt.

DIANA *is almost hit by emotion.*

DIANA Oh...well...goodness... That's so nauseatingly sentimental I might have to throw up. And shouldn't I be dead before I'm immortalised?

SARAH I'll bring the cyanide and ground glass next time. Bye, Aunty.

DIANA Aunt. Great aunt!

SARAH *exits off the verandah with the baby in the basket.* **DIANA** *blinks and gets back to peering at her laptop.*

Prostate problems in dogs? Oh for goodness sakes. *(types)* Prostates in the elderly...

JANE *comes in and catches this.*

JANE Have you got prostate trouble, Diana?

DIANA *shakes her head in disbelief.*

DIANA Have you been in healthcare for long Jane?

JANE Oh yes, years.

DIANA Well let me add a footnote to your obviously encyclopaedic medical knowledge. Women don't have prostates.

JANE Oh...you mean all women? Not just you?

DIANA What do you think I am? Only men have prostates.

JANE Oh...well I never.

DIANA We have breasts. They are *our* smoking guns, ready to turn on us at a moment's notice. Have you checked yours recently?

JANE Oh, Diana. Please. What sort of woman do you think I am?

JANE *exits.* **DIANA** *yelling after her.*

DIANA Check for bumps and lumps, you great nitwit... God what do they teach them?

TOM *comes out of his door, taking off his coat.*

TOM Hello, old thing.

DIANA *goes to him.*

DIANA Tom... Where have you been?

TOM To the specialist.

DIANA That was hours ago. I've been going frantic here. What did he say?

TOM Didn't see him. He was called out on a golfing emergency.

DIANA So you don't know?

TOM Oh yes, I know.

DIANA Well?

TOM Yes.

DIANA Yes, what?

TOM I'm well. Going to have to shave a bit off the prostate but it's nothing deadly.

DIANA I'm so glad...so happy for you.

They hug.

You should have spoken up earlier, you great pillock.

TOM Men find it hard to talk about doodah problems. We get embarrassed.

DIANA And how do you think women feel when they get checked out? Feet in stirrups, five hundred medical students with binoculars and crisps in the front row. Eh? We grin and bear it because we know we can't afford to get embarrassed. If you get embarrassed, you end up snuffing it before your time. Bloody old fool. I need a drink.

DIANA *heads for the booze.* **TOM** *reflects and watches* **DIANA.**

What?

TOM Diana... You're very good at it you, know.

DIANA Well I learnt a lot by sleeping around as a young woman.

TOM I didn't mean that. I meant at getting ideas across. Crusading. You get things done by sheer bombast and aggression.

DIANA Thank you. I think.

TOM But is it the right way? Or would you get just as much done if you'd worked with your heart rather than your spleen and boots?

DIANA I don't know. Your stupid question.

TOM That's the point. I don't know either. I don't know whether you're wonderful or awful.

DIANA Does it matter?

TOM No. Not at all. Because I know that whether you're wonderfully awful or awfully wonderful, right or wrong... I'm sure of one thing... I love you very much.

DIANA *stops and turns. They hold a look. Eventually* **DIANA** *turns away and goes and sits with her drink. Looking a bit gloomy.*

Diana?

DIANA That's very kind and I thank you and...yes...okay...I love you too. You are an ally, a mate.

TOM Is that all?

DIANA *looks uncomfortable.*

DIANA Tom... What is life?

TOM Oh God, I don't know. That's a bit deep for cocktail hour.

DIANA Life is a short walk between two dark places.

TOM She said, looking on the bright side.

DIANA We're on our own when we arrive here and we're even more on our own when we leave.

TOM But you don't have to be alone when you go.

DIANA Yes you do. Unless you're in a bus crash.

TOM But two people can become as one.

DIANA What? How?

TOM How do you think?

DIANA I don't know, Tom. What are you saying?

TOM Oh sod it. Diana, will you marry me?

DIANA *splutters and chokes all over the place.*

I would go down on one knee but the old arthritis... Are you alright, old thing?

DIANA I think so.

TOM A coronary wasn't quite the response I was trying to elicit.

DIANA This is a bit unexpected.

TOM Seemed like the next logical step. We meet, get on, sleep together...

DIANA Then maybe bump into each other in Hong Kong or New York somewhere.

TOM Not always, Diana. To some people the next logical step is to get married.

DIANA I've heard of such people.

TOM Do you want time to think about it?

DIANA Yes. That might be a good idea.

TOM How long do you need?

DIANA Thirty years?

TOM Diana.

DIANA I need as long as I need.

TOM Okay but try not to take too long. We've brought the elephant into the room now. Can't ignore it. It's done a poo the size of a sofa.

TOM *strides off.* **DIANA** *sits in her chair and stares out. Her face tells us nothing.*

Fade lights down.

Scene Four A

Dining room.

Evening. **HARVEY** *is sitting at a table in the dining room on his mobile.*

HARVEY Yes, yes, that's the one... The Pride of the Caribbean Cruise? How much for the honeymoon suite? Uhuh...uhuh... okay...okay...and how much for a second class room down by the engines? No, forget it. I think I'll fly.

JANE *enters.*

Evening, Jane.

JANE Harvey. So, where are we going for dinner?

HARVEY Well...here.

JANE Where?

HARVEY Here, Jane. Why would we go out when we've got a fully functioning kitchen right here?

JANE Oh.

HARVEY But do sit down. I want to talk to you.

JANE Yes, Harvey?

HARVEY Now before you start cooking, I've been thinking about my career and my general position in society round here and there's one thing I've decided is a necessary addendum to my curriculum vitae.

JANE And what might that be?

HARVEY I think you were probably right about me needing a wife.

JANE Oh I'm sure I was. It would be the making of you.

HARVEY So we're agreed. Harvey needs a wife.

JANE Yes, yes, yes!

HARVEY So who do you recommend?

JANE What?

HARVEY What about that big woman down at the pub? Chris... Christine?

JANE Christopher. That's a man, Harvey. He just dresses as a woman.

HARVEY Oh... How about the masseuse down the gym? The one who cracks walnuts with her buttocks?

JANE Oh yes. That would go down really well in the golf club dining room.

HARVEY Can you think of anyone?

JANE Oh, Harvey!

JANE *gets upset.*

HARVEY What is it?

JANE *lets rip.*

JANE I've had it with you. Up to here. I've slaved away for you for years. I've saved your job, I've kept Bayview out of the papers, and what do I get in return? Nothing, nothing, nothing!

HARVEY *looks at her in amazement.*

HARVEY Jane...correct me if I'm wrong but are you a little bit upset?

JANE Harvey. I'm going to leave Bayview.

HARVEY Wait. Hang on, you can't do that. I've just had a much better idea.

JANE What?

HARVEY Well you have a job, you can fill in all the forms and you're halfway presentable so I was wondering...

JANE What?

HARVEY I was wondering if you might make a decent sort of golf club bloke's wife. So what do you say?

JANE *looks at him, pauses, then reaches out and touches him.*

Jane, you're touching me.

JANE Yes, Harvey.

She smiles and leaves her hand on him. He looks bleak and the lights fade.

Scene Five

Conservatory.

Fade back up... Three weeks later. **JANE** *comes in and bustles then stops and looks at* **DIANA**.

JANE What are you doing, Diana?

DIANA Nothing.

JANE But what nothing?

DIANA Nothing, nothing.

JANE But you must be doing something. You're always doing something. Never nothing or nothing nothing.

DIANA Jane...

JANE You're still thinking about it, aren't you? You've been sitting there for three weeks now.

DIANA Just sod off and leave me alone.

JANE I never had to think about it. As soon as Harvey even hinted I was right in there with a big fat yes, yes, yes.

DIANA Because you're a throwback to the days when women were whimpering little gobs in bonnets...while I am a fully evolved woman who has never before had to encompass the idea of a binding relationship with anything more demanding than a stuffed ferret.

JANE You mean Tom is the first person to propose to you?

DIANA The first sober person.

JANE But you never said yes?

DIANA Not to the marriage bit. I was up for the swinging from the rafters bit because I knew it would all be over by breakfast. But marriage. God, some of them last for months.

JANE Well I just want to say I think it's lovely. Tom proposing to you all over the place. The skywriting. How romantic was that?

DIANA The pilot was dyslexic. Letters a mile high. Diana, will you bury me.

JANE The ring in your champagne glass?

DIANA Four days to recover the damn thing and I'm certainly not wearing it now.

JANE Harvey's set a date for us. Maybe it's a sign for you.

DIANA When I start taking life guidance from the cretin Baines you may string me up by my few remaining testicles.

JANE So what are you going to do?

DIANA I know what I'm going to say. I'm going to say...

GEOFFREY *(offstage)* Helloooo.

DIANA Oh fuck.

> **GEOFFREY** *comes out with a bunch of flowers. Peers into* **TOM**'*s place.*

GEOFFREY Dad, Dad? Have I missed him?

JANE He said he'd see you there.

DIANA Geoffrey, you've brought us flowers. How kind.

GEOFFREY Er no... They're for my mother.

DIANA Maggie? Your father's wife?

GEOFFREY Yes.

DIANA You're taking her flowers?

GEOFFREY It's her birthday.

DIANA But she's no longer with us.

GEOFFREY No...

DIANA Am I missing something here?

GEOFFREY Every year on her birthday Dad and I take flowers to her grave.

JANE Oh isn't that lovely. One day I'll do that for Harvey.

DIANA Geoffrey, can I borrow your flowers?

GEOFFREY I don't think so, Diana, because if you take my flowers then I won't have any flowers.

DIANA I was just being polite. Come on.

DIANA *snatches his flowers and walks off.*

GEOFFREY Diana...

Scene Six

Graveyard.

An hour later. **TOM** *is by a grave looking down at his wife's headstone. Birds twitter.*

TOM Thing is, Maggie, for the last fifteen years you've always been here with me. Still. You've shared my adventures, you've stuck by me. While our Geoffrey bored me silly and his wife tried to poison me, you were always there. And you will always be here with me, for me...

DIANA *appears unseen by* **TOM**, *clutching her flowers, and watches and listens.*

...but now I've found someone else to share my adventures with. Not instead of you but as well as with you. We could be a sort of threesome...musketeers...all for one and one for...

(cont.) I know you'll be saying "Oh for gods sake Tom get on with it, I'm dead and she's alive, grab her before she conks out, you can't faff about at your age..." You and she sound a lot alike actually...but I just wanted to double-check with you... See, I can't believe I've been so lucky in my life partners... I've found another you, Maggie. I'm really happy again...really happy.

DIANA *comes alongside him and puts her flowers next to his, links an arm through his and looks up at him.*

DIANA Okay.

Scene Seven

TOM'*s conservatory.*

Two days later. **JANE** *is putting flowers on* **TOM**'*s table.* **HARVEY** *enters with a bottle of cava.*

HARVEY Well, well, wonderful news, Jane. My two favourite residents getting married. Time to break out the cava because they'll be leaving now, won't they? Buying a little cottage to see out their final tragic years. I'm so happy I could kiss a goat.

JANE Harvey! They're not leaving. They're moving in together. Here.

HARVEY Jane, you're touching me.

JANE Yes, Harvey, now we're engaged I'll be touching you every day.

HARVEY *looks at her for a beat then snatches back the cava and heads for the exit.*

HARVEY I hate my life.

JANE You'll get used to it.

JANE *follows him out just as* **SARAH** *and* **DIANA** *enter onto* **DIANA**'*s verandah.*

SARAH I think it's wonderful news.

DIANA Yes. Isn't it.

SARAH At last, a happy ending.

DIANA As they say in the best massage parlours.

The baby cries off.

SARAH Coming.

SARAH *exits.* **DIANA** *looks at her new ring. Sniffs it.*

DIANA I wonder what all my old mates would say... Not a lot, most of them being dead.

TOM *(offstage)* Come on, Geoffy, bring the glasses.

TOM *enters from his place with a bottle of champagne with* **GEOFFREY** *following him with champagne glasses.* **TOM** *pops the champagne.*

Olé...our first bottle of champers as an engaged couple.

DIANA Wonderful.

TOM So what do you think, Geoffy? Your old dad getting married again?

GEOFFREY Gosh, marriage, eh? I don't know, Dad. I remember walking down the aisle with Marion...well I was walking, she was sort of twitching and jumping down the aisle owing to a rather nasty yeast infection she got off a Jehovah's Witness. Looking back, I think that if there'd been an earthquake on that day and the whole of Hampshire had disappeared down a big hole then by now I would hardly be even a small blip on the collective memory of mankind, let alone still being married to a screaming psycho who drinks a tanker of gin every week and has slept with every upright male within a fifty-mile radius of Bournemouth and made my life so miserable that I want to throw myself off the nearest cliff and... Actually, I'm probably not the right person to ask about marriage. Bye, Dad.

TOM I'll see you out.

TOM *exits.* **DIANA** *sits in a chair. She picks up an old photo album and looks through it.*

DIANA Me with Gaddaffi. Me with Saddam. Me with Bill Clinton... *(She peers closer.)* At least I think that's me down there... Me and Tony Blair.

She looks at that one for a beat then plucks it out and chucks it over her shoulder.

A big book of memories. A catalogue of events, moments in a life... Who was I? A passing soul...no direction known, a complete unknown...

TOM *dissolves back in.*

TOM ...Like a rolling stone.

DIANA Like a rolling stone.

TOM But not anymore.

DIANA No...not anymore.

TOM Not getting cold feet, are you?

DIANA *holds his look for a beat. Then takes his hand.*

DIANA No, Tom. You've helped me make a decision I could have never made on my own.

They hug. **JANE** *runs on.*

JANE Oh Diana. Disaster.

DIANA What?

JANE Dennis has booked both our weddings at the same time.

DIANA Well tell him to change it.

JANE He can't. He's a got a funeral straight after. We're going to have to get married together.

JANE *runs off again.*

DIANA A mass wedding. We're not bloody North Korea. Come on, Jane, let's go and give Rev. Dennis a good kicking.

DIANA *strides off.* **TOM** *is left standing there. He looks up. Cups his ear.*

TOM Maggie... Maggie, are you laughing?

Scene Eight

Church.

Two weeks later. We hear pre-wedding sounds and voices. Church bells, cars arriving, car doors slamming.

Dithery **REV. DENNIS SPARROW** *totters in and looks around him. He has a big diary in his hand.*

DENNIS Wednesday...what's happening on Wednesday? Or is it Thursday. Where's my diary...oh dear... The Lord giveth and the Lord taketh away...wish he'd maketh up his mindeth.

HARVEY *enters.*

HARVEY You ready, Dennis?

DENNIS Absolutely. What for?

HARVEY The weddings.

DENNIS Oh really, you're getting married. What does Jane think about that?

HARVEY She's thrilled to bits.

DENNIS Yes, I suppose she would be. Who are you marrying?

HARVEY Jane! Get it together, Dennis. After us it's Diana and Tom.

HARVEY *exits as an* **UNDERTAKER** *in a black suit enters.*

UNDERTAKER Morning.

DENNIS Ah... Another wedding?

UNDERTAKER Funeral, Dennis, funeral. Got to set up before the punters arrive.

DENNIS Jolly good.

UNDERTAKER Can I bring him in then?

DENNIS Lovely idea.

The **UNDERTAKER** *exits.*

Let's have some music, shall we? Away you go, Mrs Williams.

He waves up at the organist. Organ music; the wedding march. **DIANA** *sticks her head round the scenery.*

DIANA *(offstage)* No one's ready yet.

DENNIS I can't stop Mrs Williams once she's started.

DIANA *(offstage)* Harvey, Jane, get out there.

HARVEY *hastens on.*

HARVEY Hurry up, Jane.

JANE *processes on in her full meringue wedding outfit and milks it.* **HARVEY** *looks aghast.*

Oh God. I'm not doing this. I've changed my mind.

JANE *grabs him and twirls him towards* **DENNIS**.

JANE Come on, Harvey.

DENNIS Hello. How are you? Who are you?

JANE Get on with it, Dennis. We've only got five minutes.

DENNIS Er...we are gathered here today to...to...er... What are we doing?

JANE Bloody wedding, Dennis.

DENNIS To bloody wedding, Dennis... No, no that doesn't sound right.

The **UNDERTAKER** *wheels the coffin on.*

UNDERTAKER Put him here then, can I?

JANE No you can't. Get out.

UNDERTAKER You've got four minutes.

UNDERTAKER *wheels the coffin off again.*

DENNIS Right. Let's proceed.

HARVEY No... Let's not.

DENNIS What?

HARVEY I can't do this.

JANE Harvey.

HARVEY I'm sorry, Jane. Taxi.

HARVEY *runs off upstage.*

JANE Harvey!

JANE *tackles* **HARVEY**. *Then turns him on his back, sits astride him, pulls him to the sitting position and punches him.*

HARVEY Ow.

HARVEY *lies back down.*

JANE Oh God, I've killed him. Don't worry, Harvey. I'll save you. Kiss of life!

JANE *lies on top of* **HARVEY**. *Kissing him as he waves frantically from underneath her.* **JANE** *briefly looks back.*

You carry on, Dennis.

DENNIS *looks at his notes as* **JANE** *snogs* **HARVEY** *into the floor.*

DENNIS Er... Next...Mr and Mrs Ballard to be. Tom and Diana.

TOM *and* **DIANA** *step out upstage in all their wedding finery.* **GEOFFREY, SARAH** *and baby with them.*

Start again, Mrs Williams.

The **UNDERTAKER** *rolls the coffin on again. The organist starts to play the funeral march.*

DIANA Oh bloody hell. Gwyneth! Wedding march. And you get the hell out of here.

UNDERTAKER Oh very nice. Thank you.

UNDERTAKER *wheels coffin off again.*

DIANA Jane, for God's sake. You're in church.

JANE Sorry Diana. Come along, Harvey. Up you get. We'll do ours after the funeral.

JANE *gets the dazed* **HARVEY** *to his feet and becomes part of the back-up gang.*

The **UNDERTAKER** *briefly sticks her head out.*

UNDERTAKER Punters are here. Two minutes.

DENNIS Bit of a time problem, Mrs Williams.

The organ plays the wedding march at double quick time.

DIANA Oh for God's sake.

DIANA *grabs* **TOM** *and quickly marches him up to* **DENNIS.**

Hold it, Gywneth!

The music stops.

Go, Dennis.

DENNIS Okay. What?

DIANA *snatches his prayer book from* **DENNIS** *and pulls out her own service sheet.*

DIANA Just read this. I've cut the boring bits so start there.

DENNIS Oh right... Do you, Diana Trent, take this man, Tom Ballard, to be your lawfully wedded husband, to have and to hold from this day forward; for better, for worse, for richer, for poorer, in sickness and in health, to love and to cherish, till death do you part?

DIANA Yes... Yes... I do.

DENNIS Oh, isn't that nice?

DIANA Next bit.

DENNIS Do you, Thomas Edward Ballard, take this woman, Diana Trent, to be your lawfully wedded wife to have and to hold from this day forward; for better, for worse, for richer, for poorer, in sickness and in health, to love and to cherish, till death do you part?

TOM *turns to* **DIANA** *and takes her hands in his, they look at each other for a long pause.*

Did I get that right?

DIANA Get on with it, Tom.

TOM What?

DIANA Answer the bloody question.

TOM What was the question?

DIANA Oh dear God. Dennis. Again.

DENNIS Do you, Tom, take Diana as your awfully wedded... lawfully wedded wife?

TOM *looks around the church. Thinks for a moment.*

DIANA Tom?

TOM Yes, Diana.

DIANA Well do you?

TOM Um... I don't think so...no.

Gasps all round.

GEOFFREY Dad, this is where you say I do.

TOM But I don't.

DIANA Tom, what is going on?

TOM Diana, I think it's a terrible idea.

DIANA What?

TOM I think it would ruin everything. I think we have it all the way we are. Why risk it all just to "satisfy some dreadful petit bourgeois feudal bollocks aimed at tying women to the sink and reducing them to chattels". As one very wise woman once said. Terrible idea.

DIANA *steps back and looks at him with a big smile.*

DIANA You bastard.

TOM I'm so sorry if I'm breaking your heart and leaving you abandoned at the altar. Please forgive me, Miss Havisham.

DIANA You knew. You wicked old goat, you knew. I adore you.

They hug. **TOM** *hands a piece of paper to* **DENNIS**.

TOM Read.

DENNIS I now declare you... NOT man and wife... I declare you... Tom and Diana.

DIANA Tom.

TOM And Diana.

DENNIS Tom and Diana.

ALL Tom and Diana!

ALL *applaud and cheer and* **TOM** *and* **DIANA** *exit to the Trumpet Voluntary with the rest of the cast following and showering them with confetti.*

The **UNDERTAKER** *wheels the coffin on.* **DENNIS** *returns and looks at the coffin and flowers.*

DENNIS Harvest festival?

Blackout. Curtain.

PROPS

ACT ONE

Set of outdoor furniture: simple table and two chairs	p.1
Pack of playing cards	p.1
Clipboard (**JANE**)	p.2
Walking stick (**DIANA**)	p.2
Yellow waistcoat and bow tie (**TOM**)	p.8
Clipboard and pen (**HARVEY**)	p.9
Book (**DIANA**)	p.12
Soup for all, bowls, cutlery etc	p.13
Food to be delivered by maid	p.14
Airgun (**DIANA**)	p.17
Book (**DIANA**)	p.17
Porsche car keys	p.20
Two plates of food (**SARAH**)	p.25
Sunglasses	p.25
Zimmer frame	p.30
Newspaper	p.33
Bunches of flowers and a vase	p.33
Stick (**DIANA**)	p.34
Mobile phone	p.35
Bag of ice (**HARVEY**)	p.39
Knitting needles, wool, knitted tube (bootie)	p.40
Gin and a mug	p.40
Tray of tea	p.44
Black gauze	p.45
Oxygen mask	p.45
Wrapped baby	p.46

ACT TWO

Cup of tea	p.48
Empty bottles	p.48
Newspapers	p.53

Paper pad and pen (**DR HENRY**)	p.57
Laptop (**DIANA**)	p.59
Baby in crib	p.59
Baby blanket, basket	p.60
Coat (**TOM**)	p.61
Booze	p.62
Mobile phone (**HARVEY**)	p.65
Bunch of flowers (**GEOFFREY**)	p.69
Bottle of cava	p.72
Ring (**DIANA**)	p.72
Bottle of champagne and glasses	p.73
Old photo album	p.73
Big diary (**REV. DENNIS**)	p.75
Coffin	p.76
Notes (**REV. DENNIS**)	p.77
Coffin	p.77
Prayer book and service sheet	p.78
Confetti	p.80

SOUND EFFECTS

Fade music, bring up birdsong	p.1
Bring up birdsong a fraction	p.1
Gunshots (**DIANA**)	p.17
More gunshots (**DIANA**)	p.19
Roar of a Porsche starting up	p.21
Screech of tyres	p.21
Screech of tyres as car slides to a halt	p.22
Doors slam	p.22
Gulls cry	p.22
Crashing sound from off	p.27
Sound of ambulance	p.35
Ambulance siren, doors slamming, people calling, rattle of a hospital trolley	p.44
Baby howling	p.46
Loo flush (offstage)	p.54
Loo flush again (offstage)	p.54
Loo flush (offstage)	p.56
Baby whimpering noises	p.59
Baby gurgles	p.59
Baby cries (offstage)	p.72
Pre-wedding sounds and voices	p.75
Church bells, cars arriving, car doors slamming	p.75
Organ music (the wedding march)	p.76
Organ music (the funeral march)	p.77
Organ music (the wedding march at double quick time)	p.78
Music stops	p.78
Trumpet Voluntary	p.80

Milton Keynes UK
Ingram Content Group UK Ltd.
UKHW022224180924
448454UK00012B/302